WordPerfect® 6.0 for Windows™

Shortcuts!™

by

MICROREF®

Educational Systems, Inc.
Northbrook, Illinois U.S.A.

Product Number C250

97 96 95 94 4 3

Printed in the United States of America

WELCOME!

Welcome to the speediest guide to computer software. Our goal is to save you time.

Many pull-down menus have quick and easy keyboard or mouse alternatives. This guide reveals those hidden shortcuts!

In addition to critical menu commands, you will find time-saving keyboard and mouse tricks that speed you through your work. Have you ever said to yourself, "One day I will learn those icons so that I can actually use them"? The most useful icons are included here along with keyboard alternatives.

See how many shortcuts you can memorize. If you have learned many shortcuts already, glance over this easy-to-use, functional guide to find those lesser-known keys.

We hope you will experience those "ah-ha" moments we had in writing this guide. We encourage you to pick up other Microref Shortcuts™ guides to save time with the rest of your software programs!

CONTENTS

START AND EXIT

Start WordPerfect........................ 2CLICK

Go to next program .... **Alt Esc**

Cycle through programs .... **Alt Tab**
Hold down Alt and press Tab repeatedly until the open program that you want to use appears.

Manage open programs....................... **Ctrl Esc**
Go to a different program, close a program, or show all open programs on the screen.

Exit WordPerfect........... **Alt F4** *or* 2CLICK

MENUS

Access menu.. **Alt** *or* **F10**

Access QuickMenu................. RCLICK **object**
Click on parts of the screen or objects such as a block of text, table, or graphic.

Document menu.............................. **Alt -** *or*

Application menu.............. **Alt Spacebar** *or*

Cancel command.................... **Esc** *or* **Alt** *or* **F10**

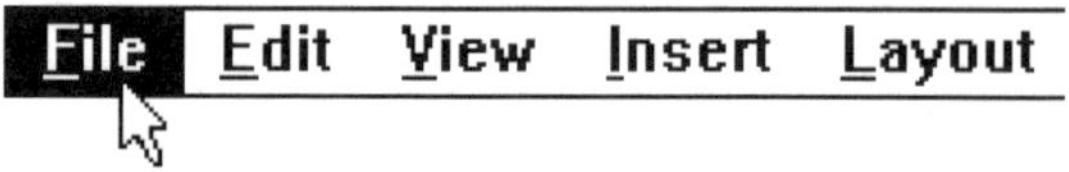

File Edit View Insert Layout

Open and Close

Open a document .... Ctrl O *or*

Create new document .... Ctrl N *or*

Create doc. from template (page 25) ...... Ctrl T

Close document .... Ctrl F4 *or* 2CLICK

Clear screen (no save) .... Ctrl Shift F4

Save with new name or file format F3

Save document .... Ctrl S *or*

Save all documents .... Ctrl Shift S

Print

Print document (from dialog box) ..... F5 *or*

Print entire document .... Ctrl P

Print envelope (select address first) ....

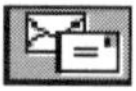

File Edit View Insert Layout

Undo

Undo last action .... Ctrl Z *or* [Undo button]

Undoes last edit, format, deletion, or command. Repeat to return to original.

Undelete..Ctrl Shift Z

Restores text to the cursor position. Undelete up to 3 previous deletions (Next, Previous).

Move the Cursor

Previous word .... Ctrl ←

Next word .... Ctrl →

Beginning of line ....Home

End of line.. End

Previous page.....................................Alt PgUp

Next page..Alt PgDn

Top of file.......................................Ctrl Home

End of file..Ctrl End

Go to page .... Ctrl G

Mark your place (QuickMark) .... Ctrl Shift Q

Return to place (QuickMark).................... Ctrl Q

Move Before Codes

Beginning of line .... Home Home

Top of file......................... Ctrl Home Ctrl Home

Edit Codes

Reveal codes (on/off) .... **Alt F3**
Shows how your document is formatted.

Edit a code.. **2CLICK**
Double-click on a formatting code in the codes pane and a dialog box opens to edit the format (most codes).

Delete a code .... **DRAG**
Removes formatting. Drag code off pane. Or, place the cursor before the code and press Del.

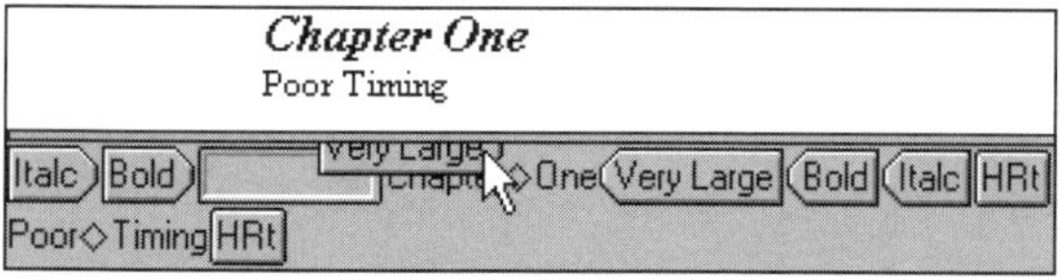

Select (Block)

Selection mode (on/off)........................... F8 →

Press F8. Then press a cursor movement key. Example: To select from the cursor to the end of the line, press F8 then press End.

Another method ....Shift →

Hold down Shift and press a cursor movement key. Example: To select to the end of the line, hold down Shift and press End.

Select with Mouse

Block .... DRAG ▯

Graphic.. CLICK ▯

Word .... 2CLICK ▯

Sentence .... 3CLICK ▯

Paragraph .... 4CLICK ▯

Line........................... Ctrl ▯ RCLICK left margin

QuickMenu .... ▯ RCLICK left margin

Beginning of block............... CLICK ▯ beginning

End of block .... Shift CLICK ▯ end

Move and Copy with Clipboard

Cut selection to Clipboard .... **Ctrl X**

Copy selection to Clipboard .... **Ctrl C**

Append selection to Clipboard .... **Alt ED**
Adds block to end of Clipboard (rather than replacing contents).

Paste .... **Ctrl V**
Inserts Clipboard contents at cursor.

Move and Copy with Mouse

Select block of text first, then:

Move .... **DRAG block**

Copy .... **Ctrl DRAG block**

Delete

Selection .... **Del**

Word .... **Ctrl Backspace**

To end of line .... **Ctrl Del**

To end of page .... **Ctrl Shift Del**

Type over (toggle "Typeover" on/off) .... **Ins**

Undelete..Ctrl Shift Z

Find and Replace

Find text/codes F2

Repeat last find (forward) ....Shift F2

Repeat last find (backward)...................... Alt F2

Replace text/codes..................................Ctrl F2

File Edit **View** Insert Layout

Modes

Page view (shows formatting) .... Alt F5

Draft view..Ctrl F5

Zoom

Zoom in/out................................Alt VZ *or* 100%

Full page ....Shift F5

Full page (on/off)...

Scroll left/right in zoom......... Ctrl PgUp/PgDn

Show or Hide

Codes (reveal codes)................................ Alt F3

Ruler.. Alt Shift F3
Set tabs, margins, indents, column widths.

Show symbols in text ....Ctrl Shift F3

Hide all bars (Esc to restore) .... Alt Shift F5

File Edit View Insert Layout

Bullets or Numbers

Insert bullet or number............... Alt IN *or*

At cursor or as you type each new paragraph.

Insert same bullet or number .... Ctrl Shift B

Bullet or number selected text................Alt IN

Symbols

Insert a special character .... Ctrl W

Memorize key combinations you use most often.
(Example: Ctrl W then 4,19 produces ¢.)

Or, from the Numeric keypad:

¼ **One-quarter .... Alt 0188**

½ **One-half..................................... Alt 0189**

© **Copyright .... Alt 0169**

™ **Trademark................................ Alt 0153**

® **Registered trademark............. Alt 0174**

Special Text

Current date ....Ctrl D *or* [calendar button]

Updating date code .... Ctrl Shift D

Page number .... Ctrl Shift P

Filename (current document) .... Alt IOF

Full pathname of file .... Alt IOP

Hyphens and Breaks

Normal hyphen (know-how)...............................-

Soft hyphen (Har-ry) .... Ctrl Shift -

Hard hyphen (332-4358) .... Ctrl -

Hard space (May 2)...................... Ctrl Spacebar

•En dash .... Alt 0150

•Em dash .... Alt 0151

Page break ....Ctrl Enter

Column break.......................................Ctrl Enter

Page break among columns....Ctrl Shift Enter

File Edit View Insert **Layout**

Default Document Formats

Select a printer first .... Alt FL
Available font and page size options depend on which printer you select. Before creating a document, select the printer you intend to use.

Set defaults............ 2CLICK Open Style: InitialStyle
Sets default formatting (such as margins and page size) for the current document. The code is at the top of the codes pane (Alt F3 to show codes).

Set default font for document .... Alt LDF

Font

Affect text following cursor or select text first:

Font ....

Size ....

Font, size, color, appearance .... F9 *or* **Ctrl F**
Opens the Font dialog box.

Copy format with mouse (on/off) ....
First select formatted text or paragraph with style.

Appearance

These formats insert paired codes. To apply these codes, either select text first or insert codes when you type new text.

Bold ⟩Title⟨ Bold

Select text first .... Shift →

Insert codes while typing .... key, text, key

"Key" refers to the following Ctrl key combinations.

Bold (on/off) .... Ctrl B

Italic (on/off) .... Ctrl I

Underline (on/off) .... Ctrl U

Tabs

Affect text following the cursor or select text first:

Show ruler .... Alt Shift F3

Delete tab .... DRAG ◣ off ruler

Move tab .... DRAG ◣ on ruler

Set tab type .... ◣L

Add tab .... CLICK ruler

First, set the tab type. Then add a tab.

Format Lines

Center rest of line .... Shift F7

Flush right rest of line................................ Alt F7

Flush right with dot leaders .... Alt F7 Alt F7

Align (Justify) Paragraphs

Align current and following paragraphs or selection.

Left .... Ctrl L

Right.. Ctrl R

Center .... Ctrl E

Full (left and right).. Ctrl J

With mouse................. HOLD and select

Indent Paragraphs

Position the cursor at beginning of paragraph.

Left indent.. F7 *or*

Hanging indent... Ctrl F7

Left and right.................................. Ctrl Shift F7

With bullet or number........Ctrl Shift B *or*

Alt IN sets the type of bullet or number.

Into left margin (release) ....Shift Tab

Format Pages

Affects pages following the cursor or select pages first.

Set margins ....Ctrl F8

Left margin (ruler) .... DRAG

Right margin (ruler)............................ DRAG

Insert a page break............................Ctrl Enter

Format with Styles

Apply style to selected text....... Alt F8 *or*

Create style from selected text.....Alt F8 Alt Q

Columns

Set up columns ....

Change width (ruler) .... DRAG *or*

Insert column break...........................Ctrl Enter

Tools Graphics Table Window

Macros

Record a macro (start/stop) ....Ctrl F10

Play a macro... Alt F10

Some time-saving macros:

ALLFONTS .... Print list of all your fonts

DROPCAPS................... Dropped capital letter

GOTODOS.................... Opens a DOS window

FILESTMP .... Print filename in header

PAGEXOFY ....Print “Page X of Y” in header

PGBORDER .... Border pages

REVERSE ......White text on black background

SQCONFIG................... Use SmartQuotes (“ ”)

Sort and Merge

Sort selected or following paragraphs .. Alt F9

Merge documents .... Shift F9

Writing Aids

Spell check .... Ctrl F1 *or* 
Checks entire document or selected text.

Thesaurus .... Alt F1 *or* 
Checks current word.

Grammar .... Alt Shift F1 *or* 
Checks entire document or selected text.

Tools **Graphics** Table Window

Straight Lines

Horizontal line .... Ctrl F11

Vertical line .... Ctrl Shift F11

Pictures

Insert a picture (figure) F11

Edit picture 2CLICK

Select picture .... CLICK

Edit picture box .... Shift F11

Access QuickMenu .... RCLICK

Move .... DRAG center

Resize .... DRAG handle

Text Boxes

Create a text box .... Alt F11

Edit text box .... Shift F11

Tools Graphics **Table** Window

Create Table

Create a table .... **F12** *or* [table button]

Insert row above .... **Alt Ins**

Insert row below .... **Alt Shift Ins**
Or, from the bottom right cell, press Tab.

Delete current row .... **Alt Del**

Select Cells

Select current cell .... **Shift F8**

Select range of cells .... **Shift →**

Select row or column .. **2CLICK** **inside border**

Move Around in a Table

By cell .... **Alt ↑ ↓ ← →**

Cell right .... **Tab**

Cell left .... **Shift Tab**

First cell in row............................Home Home

Last cell in row....................................End End

Top of cell... Alt Home

Bottom of cell...Alt End

Format Cells

Format table..Ctrl F12

Add lines and shading........................Shift F12

Format numbers (e.g., currency).......... Alt F12

Column width.......................... DRAG ▼ (ruler)

Edit a Cell

Insert tab stop in a cell....................... Ctrl Tab

Insert decimal tab.......................... Alt Shift F7

Insert back tab.......................... Ctrl Shift Tab

Sum cells (above or to the left)................Ctrl =

Fill cells based on pattern...........Ctrl Shift F12

Enter data to set pattern (e.g., Monday, Tuesday or 5, 10). Select these cells and cells to fill.

Tools Graphics Table **Window**

Arrange Document Windows

Go to next open document .... Ctrl F6

Go to previous document .... Ctrl Shift F6

Tile (show) all windows .... Alt WT

Cascade (overlap) all windows .... Alt WC

Move window .... DRAG title bar

Resize Document Windows

Zoom to fill the screen .... 2CLICK title bar

Return to original size ....

Any size .... DRAG border

Minimize to icon ....

Restore from icon 2CLICK

PRESET TEMPLATES

Documents are based on templates: text, formatting (such as margins, default font, etc.), or pictures in the template appear in the document. New documents use a template named Standard. These templates come with WordPerfect 6.0:

Create document based on template.....Ctrl T

Edit template........ Ctrl T, template, Options E

Personal Business

EXPENSE	Daily expense report for week
IDEALIST	Notebook for brainstorming
MILEAGE	Mileage record with expenses
RESUME	Standard job resume

Company Business

BALANCE	Balance sheet statement
INCOME	Income statement
INVENTOR	Keep track of inventory
QCASHFLW	Quarterly cash flow statement

Business Forms

COSTANYL	Cost analysis of project costs
CREDITAP	Commercial credit application
ESTIMATE	Job description, estimated costs
INVOICE	Standard invoice billing someone
JOBAPP	Application for employment
PACKING	Standard packing list for shipment
PRESS1/2	Press releases
PURCHASE	Standard purchase order form

Legal Forms

LEGLBILL	Billing statement for legal services
PLEADCVR	Cover sheet for legal pleading

Certificates and Signs

CERTIF1	Award, portrait
CERTIF2	Achievement, landscape
SIGN1	Art deco style sign
SIGN2	Southwestern style sign
SIGN5	Announcement (sideways)

Student

CLASSCHD	Student's class schedule
REPORT3	Schoolbook-style report
REPORT5	Standard term paper

Teacher

ATTEND	Monthly attendance roll
GRADE	Monthly student grade sheet
SIGN3	Seminar announcement
SIGN4	Lecture announcement

Phones

PHONELST	Store names and numbers
PHONEMSG	Four telephone message forms

Keeping Track of Time

CAL_SIDE	Monthly calendar (sideways)
CAL_UP	Monthly calendar (vertical)
PLANDAY	Daily planner with appointments
PLANWEEK	Weekly planner

Correspondence

ENVLPE	Business envelope
FAX1	Casual fax cover sheet
FAX2	Contemporary fax cover sheet
FAX3	Traditional fax cover sheet
FAX4	Cosmopolitan fax cover sheet
FAX5	Boxed style fax cover sheet
LETTER1	Traditional letterhead
LETTER2	Graphic letterhead
LETTER3	Standard letterhead
LETTER4	Contemporary letterhead
LETTER5	Centered traditional letterhead
MEMO1	Casual memo
MEMO2	Contemporary memo
MEMO3	Traditional memo
MEMO4	Cosmopolitan memo
MEMO5	Italic memo

Newsletters and Reports

NEWSLTR1	Newsletter with cursive title
NEWSLTR2	Newsletter with blocked title

Reports

REPORT1	Report with filename in footer
REPORT2	Report with classical capitals
REPORT4	Report in contemporary style

Title Pages

TITLEPG1	Title page with gray box at top
TITLEPG2	Title page with centered title
TITLEPG3	Title page with indented title

YOUR SHORTCUTS

Did we omit any of your favorite shortcuts?

If this book does not include a command or shortcut that you use often, write it down here. You may also want to record shortcut keys that you created yourself or jot down the names of important files.

INDEX

WORDPERFECT 6.0 FOR WINDOWS

	F1	F2	F3	F4	F5	F6
Ctrl Shift			Show ¶	Clear		Prev. Doc.
Ctrl	Speller	Replace	Redisplay	Close Doc.	Draft View	Next Doc.
Alt Shift	Grammar		Ruler On/Off		Hide Bars	Prev. Win.
Alt	Thesaurus	Find Prev.	Rev. Codes	Exit WP	Page View	Next Win.
Shift	What Is?	Find Next	Save	New Doc.	Full Page	Prev. Pane
Unshift	Help	Find	Save As	Open Doc.	Print	Next Pane

	F7	F8	F9	F10	F11	F12
Ctrl Shift	Indent L/R				Vert. Line	Table Data
Ctrl	Hang Indent	Margins	Generate	Macro Rec.	Horiz. Line	Table Format
Alt Shift	Decimal Tab			Feat. Bar		
Alt	Flush Right	Styles	Sort	Macro Play	Cr. Text Box	Table Num.
Shift	Center	Select Cell	Merge	Repeat	Ed. Text Box	Table Lines
Unshift	Indent Left	Select Mode	Font	Menu	Figure	Table Create